C000272274

HarperCollins*Publishers*
1 London Bridge Street
London SE1 9GF

www.harpercollins.co.uk

HarperCollins*Publishers*
1st Floor, Watermarque Building, Ringsend Road
Dublin 4, Ireland

First published by HarperCollins*Publishers* 2021

13 5 7 9 10 8 6 4 2

Text © HarperCollins*Publishers* 2021
Images © Shutterstock.com

HarperCollins*Publishers* asserts the moral right to
be identified as the author of this work

A catalogue record of this book is
available from the British Library

ISBN 978-0-00-843868-5

Printed and bound in Great Britain by
CPI Group (UK) Ltd, Croydon

MIX
Paper from
responsible sources
FSC™ C007454

This book is produced from independently certified FSC™ paper
to ensure responsible forest management.

For more information visit: www.harpercollins.co.uk/green

SHAG MARRY AVOID

EVERYONE'S FAVOURITE GAME OF DILEMMAS

HarperCollins*Publishers*

Contents

Introduction

SHAG, MARRY, AVOID *could* be described as a cruel, fickle game that combines split-second decision-making with blatant objectification... But it could *also* be described as **A HELL OF A LOT OF FUN!**

Guiding you through a whole host of categories, from historical figures to film stars, music idols to secret crushes, this book provides prompts and suggestions to keep those options flying at a crucially fast pace!

This rapid-fire game is perfect for any party or gathering, or as a networking ice-breaker, and once you start playing, you won't want to stop.

So get to know your friends/family/ colleagues a little better and get ready to be **VERY** confused by some of their answers!

We provide the options. The decisions are up to you ...

FILM

& TV
STARS

From big-screen legends to small-screen royalty, whether you prefer the glamour of an Oscar-winner, the rugged style of a *Game of Thrones* hero or the magic of a Hogwarts alumnus, they are all here for you to choose from ...

HANDSOME HOTSHOTS

Chris Pratt

Idris Elba

Will Smith

ACTION HEROINES

Angelina Jolie

Jessica Alba

Scarlett Johansson

ACTION HEROES

Tom Cruise

Russell Crowe

Matt Damon

CREATIVE QUEENS

	👄	💍	⚠️
Michaela Coel	☐	☐	☐
Phoebe Waller-Bridge	☐	☐	☐
Sharon Horgan	☐	☐	☐

BATTLE OF THE RYANS

	👄	💍	⚠️
Ryan Gosling	☐	☐	☐
Ryan Reynolds	☐	☐	☐
Ryan Seacrest	☐	☐	☐

AWARD-WINNERS

	👄	💍	⚠️
Awkwafina	☐	☐	☐
Lupita Nyong'o	☐	☐	☐
Saoirse Ronan	☐	☐	☐

'Love at
first sight?
I absolutely
believe in it!
You've got
to keep the
faith.'

LEONARDO
DICAPRIO

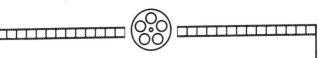

KIND OF A BIG DEAL

⌣ 💍 ⚠

Leonardo DiCaprio

☐☐☐

Channing Tatum

☐☐☐

Chris Hemsworth

☐☐☐

AWESOME AUSSIES

⌣ 💍 ⚠

Margot Robbie

☐☐☐

Rebel Wilson

☐☐☐

Isla Fisher

☐☐☐

STAR WARS STARS

⌣ 💍 ⚠

Riz Ahmed

☐☐☐

Adam Driver

☐☐☐

John Boyega

☐☐☐

FUNNY WOMEN

	👄	💍	⚠
Tina Fey	☐	☐	☐
Amy Poehler	☐	☐	☐
Kristen Wiig	☐	☐	☐

HOGWARTS ALUMNI

	👄	💍	⚠
Daniel Radcliffe	☐	☐	☐
Robert Pattinson	☐	☐	☐
Tom Felton	☐	☐	☐

MAMMA MIA!

	👄	💍	⚠
Lily James	☐	☐	☐
Amanda Seyfried	☐	☐	☐
Meryl Streep	☐	☐	☐

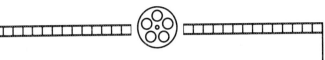

ROMANTIC LEADS

                  👄 💍 ⚠️

James McAvoy ☐ ☐ ☐

Dominic Cooper ☐ ☐ ☐

Colin Firth ☐ ☐ ☐

BIG-SCREEN BABES

                  👄 💍 ⚠️

Jennifer Lawrence ☐ ☐ ☐

Amy Schumer ☐ ☐ ☐

Emma Stone ☐ ☐ ☐

BOND, JAMES BOND

                  👄 💍 ⚠️

Pierce Brosnan ☐ ☐ ☐

Daniel Craig ☐ ☐ ☐

Timothy Dalton ☐ ☐ ☐

'LOVE IS DOING SOMETHING YOU DON'T WANT TO DO FOR SOMEONE YOU DON'T PARTICULARLY LIKE AT THAT MOMENT.'

TOM HARDY

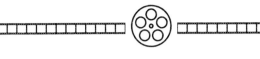

BOND GIRLS

                                           👄 💍 ⚠

Halle Berry ☐ ☐ ☐

Grace Jones ☐ ☐ ☐

Gemma Arterton ☐ ☐ ☐

HUGH'S RIGHT FOR YOU?

👄 💍 ⚠

Hugh Grant ☐ ☐ ☐

Hugh Laurie ☐ ☐ ☐

Hugh Jackman ☐ ☐ ☐

LEADING LADIES

👄 💍 ⚠

Penelope Cruz ☐ ☐ ☐

Cate Blanchett ☐ ☐ ☐

Julia Roberts ☐ ☐ ☐

SHERLOCK

	💋	💍	⚠
Martin Freeman	☐	☐	☐
Benedict Cumberbatch	☐	☐	☐
Andrew Scott	☐	☐	☐

EVA 4EVA

	💋	💍	⚠
Eva Mendes	☐	☐	☐
Eva Longoria	☐	☐	☐
Eva Green	☐	☐	☐

MOVIE MUSCLE MEN

	💋	💍	⚠
Bruce Willis	☐	☐	☐
Arnold Schwarzenegger	☐	☐	☐
Dwayne Johnson	☐	☐	☐

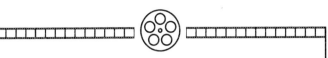

LOVABLE LEADS   👄 💍 ⚠️

George Clooney   □ □ □

Bradley Cooper   □ □ □

Jude Law   □ □ □

BRIGHT YOUNG THINGS   👄 💍 ⚠️

Timothée Chalamet   □ □ □

Ansel Elgort   □ □ □

Michael Cera   □ □ □

FIGHT CLUB   👄 💍 ⚠️

Edward Norton   □ □ □

Brad Pitt   □ □ □

Jared Leto   □ □ □

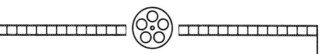

JAMIE, JAMIE, JAMIE   👄 💍 ⚠️

Jamie Bell

Jamie Foxx

Jamie Dornan

HOLLYWOOD PRINCES   👄 💍 ⚠️

Marlon Brando

James Dean

John Wayne

HOLLYWOOD PRINCESSES   👄 💍 ⚠️

Marilyn Monroe

Grace Kelly

Audrey Hepburn

GoT QUEENS

Emilia Clarke

Sophie Turner

Nathalie Emmanuel

GoT KINGS

Kit Harington

Jason Momoa

Richard Madden

ACADEMY AWARD-WINNERS

Olivia Colman

Renée Zellweger

Viola Davis

TOM, TOM, TOM

👄 💍 ⚠

Tom Hanks ☐☐☐

Tom Hardy ☐☐☐

Tom Hiddleston ☐☐☐

CHARLIE'S ANGELS

👄 💍 ⚠

Lucy Liu ☐☐☐

Drew Barrymore ☐☐☐

Cameron Diaz ☐☐☐

TV LEGENDS

👄 💍 ⚠

Kiefer Sutherland ☐☐☐

Damian Lewis ☐☐☐

Blair Underwood ☐☐☐

DOCTOR WHO?

☙ ♔ ⚠

Matt Smith ☐ ☐ ☐

David Tennant ☐ ☐ ☐

Peter Capaldi ☐ ☐ ☐

DUMBLEDORE v GANDALF

☙ ♔ ⚠

Ian McKellen ☐ ☐ ☐

Michael Gambon ☐ ☐ ☐

Richard Harris ☐ ☐ ☐

WICKED WITCHES

☙ ♔ ⚠

Emma Thompson ☐ ☐ ☐

Julie Walters ☐ ☐ ☐

Imelda Staunton ☐ ☐ ☐

POLITICIANS &

PUBLIC FIGURES

From sporting legends to royals, prime ministers to billionaires, who would share your Uber Eats, entertain you between the sheets or find themselves out on the street? You decide ...

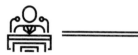

INFAMOUS LEADERS

                              👄 💍 ⚠️

Name	👄	💍	⚠️
Donald Trump	☐	☐	☐
Vladimir Putin	☐	☐	☐
Boris Johnson	☐	☐	☐

DEMOCRATS

Name	👄	💍	⚠️
Joe Biden	☐	☐	☐
Barack Obama	☐	☐	☐
Bernie Sanders	☐	☐	☐

ROYAL PRINCES

Name	👄	💍	⚠️
Prince William	☐	☐	☐
Prince Harry	☐	☐	☐
Prince Charles	☐	☐	☐

TECH BILLIONAIRES

Mark Zuckerberg

Bill Gates

Elon Musk

FOOTBALL MANAGERS

José Mourinho

Jürgen Klopp

Arsène Wenger

WHO RUNS THE WORLD?

Jacinda Ardern

Angela Merkel

Michelle Obama

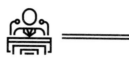

FOOTBALL LEGENDS

Frank Lampard

David Beckham

Thierry Henry

TENNIS CHAMPIONS

Serena Williams

Maria Sharapova

Venus Williams

WIMBLEDON WINNERS

Roger Federer

Novak Djokovic

Rafael Nadal

WORLD NUMBER ONES   👄 💍 ⚠

Mo Farah   ☐ ☐ ☐

Usain Bolt   ☐ ☐ ☐

Michael Phelps   ☐ ☐ ☐

ROYAL PRINCESSES   👄 💍 ⚠

Catherine, Duchess of Cambridge   ☐ ☐ ☐

Meghan Markle   ☐ ☐ ☐

Princess Beatrice of York   ☐ ☐ ☐

POLITICAL LEADERS   👄 💍 ⚠

Justin Trudeau   ☐ ☐ ☐

Emmanuel Macron   ☐ ☐ ☐

Pedro Sánchez   ☐ ☐ ☐

'The only
time you run out
of chances
is when you
stop taking
them.'

DAVID
BECKHAM

PROMINENT TORIES

👄 💍 ⚠️

Sajid Javid

☐ ☐ ☐

Rishi Sunak

☐ ☐ ☐

Dominic Cummings

☐ ☐ ☐

FORMER PARTY LEADERS

👄 💍 ⚠️

Gordon Brown

☐ ☐ ☐

David Cameron

☐ ☐ ☐

Nick Clegg

☐ ☐ ☐

LABOUR LEADERS

👄 💍 ⚠️

Jeremy Corbyn

☐ ☐ ☐

Keir Starmer

☐ ☐ ☐

Ed Miliband

☐ ☐ ☐

WOMEN IN POWER

Melania Trump

Hillary Clinton

Kamala Harris

F1 DRIVERS

Lewis Hamilton

Sebastian Vettel

Nico Rosberg

GOLFERS

Tiger Woods

Rory McIlroy

Dustin Johnson

'You can't make decisions based on fear and the possibility of what might happen.'

MICHELLE
OBAMA

BOXERS

	👄	💍	⚠
Tyson Fury	☐	☐	☐
Anthony Joshua	☐	☐	☐
Ricky Hatton	☐	☐	☐

BUSINESSMEN

	👄	💍	⚠
Alan Sugar	☐	☐	☐
Philip Green	☐	☐	☐
Richard Branson	☐	☐	☐

MODELS

	👄	💍	⚠
Naomi Campbell	☐	☐	☐
Gigi Hadid	☐	☐	☐
Kate Moss	☐	☐	☐

ASTOUNDING ATHLETES   👄 💍 ⚠️

Jessica Ennis-Hill   ☐ ☐ ☐

Kelly Holmes   ☐ ☐ ☐

Katarina Johnson-Thompson   ☐ ☐ ☐

BREXIT BOYS   👄 💍 ⚠️

Michel Barnier   ☐ ☐ ☐

Donald Tusk   ☐ ☐ ☐

Arron Banks   ☐ ☐ ☐

CRICKETERS   👄 💍 ⚠️

Stuart Broad   ☐ ☐ ☐

Ben Stokes   ☐ ☐ ☐

James Anderson   ☐ ☐ ☐

SPIRITUAL LEADERS

⬷ ŏ ⚠

Dalai Lama

Pope

Archbishop of Canterbury

SOCCER SENSATIONS

⬷ ŏ ⚠

Cristiano Ronaldo

Lionel Messi

Neymar da Silva Santos

RUGBY PLAYERS

⬷ ŏ ⚠

Jonny Wilkinson

Matt Dawson

Danny Cipriani

US PRESIDENTS

George Washington

Abraham Lincoln

John F. Kennedy

BRITISH PRIME MINISTERS

Margaret Thatcher

Winston Churchill

Anthony Eden

MILITARY MEN

Napoleon Bonaparte

Duke of Wellington

Horatio Nelson

MUSIC IDOLS

If music be the food of love, then pump up the volume! From rappers and DJs to pop stars and composers, music idols take many forms, but who would get *you* strutting to the dance floor?

ONE DIRECTIONERS

	👄	💍	⚠️
Harry Styles	☐	☐	☐
Niall Horan	☐	☐	☐
Zayn Malik	☐	☐	☐

POP PRINCESSES

	👄	💍	⚠️
Lizzo	☐	☐	☐
Katy Perry	☐	☐	☐
Rihanna	☐	☐	☐

UNSTOPPABLE ICONS

	👄	💍	⚠️
Drake	☐	☐	☐
Jay-Z	☐	☐	☐
Kanye West	☐	☐	☐

SASSY SINGER-SONGWRITERS 👄 💍 ⚠️

Taylor Swift ☐☐☐

Ariana Grande ☐☐☐

Camila Cabello ☐☐☐

RECORD-BREAKERS 👄 💍 ⚠️

Justin Bieber ☐☐☐

Ed Sheeran ☐☐☐

Shawn Mendes ☐☐☐

DESTINY'S CHILDREN 👄 💍 ⚠️

Kelly Rowland ☐☐☐

Beyoncé Knowles-Carter ☐☐☐

Michelle Williams ☐☐☐

NINETIES BOY BANDS

	⬭	💍	⚠
*NSYNC	☐	☐	☐
Backstreet Boys	☐	☐	☐
Take That	☐	☐	☐

NINETIES GIRL BANDS

	⬭	💍	⚠
Spice Girls	☐	☐	☐
All Saints	☐	☐	☐
Mis-Teeq	☐	☐	☐

SOLO SENSATIONS

	⬭	💍	⚠
Justin Timberlake	☐	☐	☐
Eminem	☐	☐	☐
Usher	☐	☐	☐

DAZZLING DIVAS

        👄 💍 ⚠️

Dua Lipa   ☐ ☐ ☐

Nicki Minaj   ☐ ☐ ☐

Selena Gomez   ☐ ☐ ☐

MUSIC LEGENDS

        👄 💍 ⚠️

Prince   ☐ ☐ ☐

Stevie Wonder   ☐ ☐ ☐

David Bowie   ☐ ☐ ☐

THE BEATLES

        👄 💍 ⚠️

John Lennon   ☐ ☐ ☐

Paul McCartney   ☐ ☐ ☐

Ringo Starr   ☐ ☐ ☐

'Know that
even if you do
make a wrong
decision, you're
making it for a
good reason.'

ADELE

ELECTRIFYING PERFORMERS

👄 💍 ⚠

Cardi B ☐ ☐ ☐

Megan Thee Stallion ☐ ☐ ☐

Miley Cyrus ☐ ☐ ☐

CHART-TOPPERS

👄 💍 ⚠

Bruno Mars ☐ ☐ ☐

Mark Ronson ☐ ☐ ☐

Pharrell Williams ☐ ☐ ☐

BRITISH RAPPERS

👄 💍 ⚠

Stormzy ☐ ☐ ☐

Kano ☐ ☐ ☐

Professor Green ☐ ☐ ☐

QUEENS OF THE STAGE   👄 💍 ⚠️

Adele ☐☐☐

Sia ☐☐☐

Lady Gaga ☐☐☐

DJs   👄 💍 ⚠️

Calvin Harris ☐☐☐

David Guetta ☐☐☐

Martin Garrix ☐☐☐

DISNEY COMPOSERS   👄 💍 ⚠️

Lin-Manuel Miranda ☐☐☐

Alan Menken ☐☐☐

Robert Lopez ☐☐☐

RAPPERS

👄 💍 ⚠️

A$AP Rocky ☐ ☐ ☐

Travis Scott ☐ ☐ ☐

Tyga ☐ ☐ ☐

R&B CHART-TOPPERS

👄 💍 ⚠️

Snoop Dogg ☐ ☐ ☐

P. Diddy ☐ ☐ ☐

50 Cent ☐ ☐ ☐

PIANO MEN

👄 💍 ⚠️

John Legend ☐ ☐ ☐

Jools Holland ☐ ☐ ☐

Jamie Cullum ☐ ☐ ☐

'BE A LOVER.
CHOOSE
LOVE.
GIVE
LOVE.'

HARRY STYLES

GOLDEN GUITARISTS

👄 💍 ⚠️

Jimi Hendrix ☐ ☐ ☐

Eric Clapton ☐ ☐ ☐

Jimmy Page ☐ ☐ ☐

EIGHTIES POP GROUPS

👄 💍 ⚠️

Wham! ☐ ☐ ☐

Spandau Ballet ☐ ☐ ☐

Duran Duran ☐ ☐ ☐

EUROVISION ROYALTY

👄 💍 ⚠️

ABBA ☐ ☐ ☐

Celine Dion ☐ ☐ ☐

Brotherhood of Man ☐ ☐ ☐

41

SEVENTIES ROCKERS

👄 💍 ⚠

Led Zeppelin ☐☐☐

Pink Floyd ☐☐☐

The Rolling Stones ☐☐☐

MEGASTARS

👄 💍 ⚠

Debbie Harry ☐☐☐

Dolly Parton ☐☐☐

Madonna ☐☐☐

GRAMMY-WINNERS

👄 💍 ⚠

Mary J. Blige ☐☐☐

Lauryn Hill ☐☐☐

Brandy ☐☐☐

LIFE-LONG LOVES

	💋	💍	⚠
Bruce Springsteen	☐	☐	☐
Sting	☐	☐	☐
Bob Dylan	☐	☐	☐

OPERA SINGERS

	💋	💍	⚠
Luciano Pavarotti	☐	☐	☐
Andrea Bocelli	☐	☐	☐
Alfie Boe	☐	☐	☐

ONE-HIT WONDERS

	💋	💍	⚠
PSY ('Gangnam Style')	☐	☐	☐
Vanilla Ice ('Ice Ice Baby')	☐	☐	☐
Baha Men ('Who Let the Dogs Out')	☐	☐	☐

HISTORICAL
FIGURES

These big names have gone down in history for a reason, and we like to think the reason was to secure their presence in this section of this very book. Congratulations to all who made it!

KINGS

✏ 💍 ⚠

King Henry VIII   ☐ ☐ ☐

King George VI   ☐ ☐ ☐

King Charles I   ☐ ☐ ☐

QUEENS

✏ 💍 ⚠

Queen Victoria   ☐ ☐ ☐

Queen Elizabeth I   ☐ ☐ ☐

Queen Anne   ☐ ☐ ☐

DIVORCED, BEHEADED, DIED

✏ 💍 ⚠

Catherine of Aragon   ☐ ☐ ☐

Anne Boleyn   ☐ ☐ ☐

Jane Seymour   ☐ ☐ ☐

INVENTORS

👄 💍 ⚠

Albert Einstein

☐☐☐

Alexander Bell

☐☐☐

Alfred Nobel

☐☐☐

WRITERS

👄 💍 ⚠

William Shakespeare

☐☐☐

Charles Dickens

☐☐☐

Leo Tolstoy

☐☐☐

NOVELISTS

👄 💍 ⚠

Jane Austen

☐☐☐

George Eliot

☐☐☐

Charlotte Brontë

☐☐☐

'But love is blind,
and lovers cannot
see the pretty follies
that themselves
commit.'

WILLIAM
SHAKESPEARE

LEADERS   👄 💍 ⚠

Mikhail Gorbachev ☐ ☐ ☐

Ronald Reagan ☐ ☐ ☐

François Mitterrand ☐ ☐ ☐

COMPOSERS   👄 💍 ⚠

Mozart ☐ ☐ ☐

Beethoven ☐ ☐ ☐

Chopin ☐ ☐ ☐

CLASSICAL GENIUSES   👄 💍 ⚠

Tchaikovsky ☐ ☐ ☐

Handel ☐ ☐ ☐

Wagner ☐ ☐ ☐

EMPIRE LEADERS

	👄	💍	⚠️
Genghis Khan	☐	☐	☐
Attila the Hun	☐	☐	☐
Alexander the Great	☐	☐	☐

ANCIENT ROMANS

	👄	💍	⚠️
Julius Caesar	☐	☐	☐
Crassus	☐	☐	☐
Pompey	☐	☐	☐

ANCIENT QUEENS

	👄	💍	⚠️
Boudicca	☐	☐	☐
Cleopatra	☐	☐	☐
Zenobia	☐	☐	☐

GREEK GODS

	😙	💍	⚠
Apollo	☐	☐	☐
Atlas	☐	☐	☐
Zeus	☐	☐	☐

GREEK GODDESSES

	😙	💍	⚠
Athena	☐	☐	☐
Hera	☐	☐	☐
Rhea	☐	☐	☐

ROMANTIC POETS

	😙	💍	⚠
William Blake	☐	☐	☐
William Wordsworth	☐	☐	☐
Samuel Taylor Coleridge	☐	☐	☐

NOBEL PRIZE-WINNERS

👄 💍 ⚠

Marie Curie

☐ ☐ ☐

Bertrand Russell

☐ ☐ ☐

Doris Lessing

☐ ☐ ☐

PAINTERS

👄 💍 ⚠

Vincent van Gogh

☐ ☐ ☐

Claude Monet

☐ ☐ ☐

Pierre-Auguste Renoir

☐ ☐ ☐

POPULAR ARTISTS

👄 💍 ⚠

Andy Warhol

☐ ☐ ☐

Damien Hirst

☐ ☐ ☐

Pablo Picasso

☐ ☐ ☐

'Anyone who has never made a mistake has never tried anything new.'

ALBERT EINSTEIN

SURREALISTS

                                                                          👄 💍 ⚠

Frida Kahlo ☐ ☐ ☐

Salvador Dalí ☐ ☐ ☐

René Magritte ☐ ☐ ☐

DIRECTORS

👄 💍 ⚠

Alfred Hitchcock ☐ ☐ ☐

Stanley Kubrick ☐ ☐ ☐

Federico Fellini ☐ ☐ ☐

PLAYWRIGHTS

👄 💍 ⚠

Harold Pinter ☐ ☐ ☐

Oscar Wilde ☐ ☐ ☐

Noël Coward ☐ ☐ ☐

PHILOSOPHERS

👄 💍 ⚠

Socrates

Kant

Voltaire

FASHION DESIGNERS

👄 💍 ⚠

Coco Chanel

Christian Dior

Alexander McQueen

STYLE ICONS

👄 💍 ⚠

Sophia Loren

Ava Gardner

Elizabeth Taylor

FICTIONAL CHARACTERS

Here is a selection of characters from some of the most popular TV shows, films, comics, books and musicals. Chandler, Ross or Joey is a choice you've probably contemplated before ... but what about Marge, Patty or Selma? Batman, Robin or the Joker? Prepare to be stumped.

F*R*I*E*N*D*S 1

	💋	💍	⚠️
Monica Geller	☐	☐	☐
Rachel Green	☐	☐	☐
Phoebe Buffay	☐	☐	☐

F*R*I*E*N*D*S 2

	💋	💍	⚠️
Ross Geller	☐	☐	☐
Chandler Bing	☐	☐	☐
Joey Tribbiani	☐	☐	☐

THE SIMPSONS LADS

	💋	💍	⚠️
Ned Flanders	☐	☐	☐
Sideshow Bob	☐	☐	☐
Willie MacDougall	☐	☐	☐

THE SIMPSONS SISTERS

⟷ 👄 ⚠

Marge Simpson

Patty Bouvier

Selma Bouvier

SEX AND THE CITY BOYS

⟷ 👄 ⚠

Mr Big

Steve Brady

Harry Goldenblatt

SEX AND THE CITY GALS

⟷ 👄 ⚠

Carrie Bradshaw

Miranda Hobbes

Samantha Jones

HOLY FATHERS

⬳ 💍 ⚠

The Hot Priest from *Fleabag* ☐ ☐ ☐

Father Ted ☐ ☐ ☐

The Vicar of Dibley ☐ ☐ ☐

THE PLASTICS

⬳ 💍 ⚠

Regina George ☐ ☐ ☐

Gretchen Wieners ☐ ☐ ☐

Karen Smith ☐ ☐ ☐

HOGWARTS GRADUATES

⬳ 💍 ⚠

Harry Potter ☐ ☐ ☐

Ron Weasley ☐ ☐ ☐

Dean Thomas ☐ ☐ ☐

'It's hard
to find people
who will love
you no matter
what. I was
lucky enough
to find three
of them.'

CARRIE
BRADSHAW

HARRY'S HEARTACHES

	💋	💍	⚠️
Cho Chang	☐	☐	☐
Romilda Vane	☐	☐	☐
Ginny Weasley	☐	☐	☐

SUPERHEROES

	💋	💍	⚠️
Superman	☐	☐	☐
Spiderman	☐	☐	☐
Wolverine	☐	☐	☐

SUPERHEROINES

	💋	💍	⚠️
Wonder Woman	☐	☐	☐
Black Widow	☐	☐	☐
Storm	☐	☐	☐

DC STARS
                                                  👄 💍 ⚠

Batman ☐ ☐ ☐

Robin ☐ ☐ ☐

The Joker ☐ ☐ ☐

THE WIZARD OF OZ
👄 💍 ⚠

The Scarecrow ☐ ☐ ☐

The Tin Man ☐ ☐ ☐

The Cowardly Lion ☐ ☐ ☐

TWILIGHT LADS
👄 💍 ⚠

Edward Cullen ☐ ☐ ☐

Jacob Black ☐ ☐ ☐

Emmett Cullen ☐ ☐ ☐

TWILIGHT LADIES

	👄	💍	⚠
Bella Swan	☐	☐	☐
Rosalie Hale	☐	☐	☐
Esme Cullen	☐	☐	☐

BOND'S FRIENDS & ENEMIES

	👄	💍	⚠
Blofeld	☐	☐	☐
Q	☐	☐	☐
Le Chiffre	☐	☐	☐

STAR TREK

	👄	💍	⚠
Kirk	☐	☐	☐
Spock	☐	☐	☐
McCoy	☐	☐	☐

'It's not
who I am
underneath,
but what
I do that
defines me.'

BATMAN

HAMILTON

⬯ 💍 ⚠

Angelica Schuyler ☐ ☐ ☐
Eliza Schuyler ☐ ☐ ☐
Peggy Schuyler ☐ ☐ ☐

LES MISÉRABLES 1

⬯ 💍 ⚠

Cosette ☐ ☐ ☐
Éponine ☐ ☐ ☐
Fantine ☐ ☐ ☐

LES MISÉRABLES 2

⬯ 💍 ⚠

Jean Valjean ☐ ☐ ☐
Javert ☐ ☐ ☐
Marius Pontmercy ☐ ☐ ☐

THE THREE MUSKETEERS ⬠ 💍 ⚠

Athos

Porthos

Aramis

TMNT ⬠ 💍 ⚠

Leonardo

Donatello

Raphael

STAR WARS ⬠ 💍 ⚠

Luke Skywalker

Darth Vader

Obi-Wan Kenobi

THE OC

⟨👄⟩ 💍 ⚠

Seth ☐ ☐ ☐

Ryan ☐ ☐ ☐

Caleb ☐ ☐ ☐

DAWSON'S CREEK

⟨👄⟩ 💍 ⚠

Dawson ☐ ☐ ☐

Pacey ☐ ☐ ☐

Charlie ☐ ☐ ☐

THE WIRE

⟨👄⟩ 💍 ⚠

Omar Little ☐ ☐ ☐

Stringer Bell ☐ ☐ ☐

Jimmy McNulty ☐ ☐ ☐

BREAKING BAD

Walter White

Jesse Pinkman

Hank Schrader

THE OFFICE

David Brent

Tim Canterbury

Gareth Keenan

NORMAL PEOPLE

Connell

Gareth

Jamie

TV & RADIO PERSONALITIES

Whether it's the radio DJ who gets you out of bed in the morning, the TV presenter who could make you chuckle all day long or the reality star you'd have a cracking night out with, here are some of the most popular personalities from the worlds of TV and radio.

NATIONAL TREASURES   👄 💍 ⚠️

Ant McPartlin ☐ ☐ ☐

Dec Donnelly ☐ ☐ ☐

Dermot O'Leary ☐ ☐ ☐

POPULAR PRESENTERS   👄 💍 ⚠️

Rylan Clark-Neal ☐ ☐ ☐

Paddy McGuinness ☐ ☐ ☐

Michael McIntyre ☐ ☐ ☐

RIDING THE RADIO WAVES   👄 💍 ⚠️

Zoe Ball ☐ ☐ ☐

Gemma Cairney ☐ ☐ ☐

Clara Amfo ☐ ☐ ☐

MORNING DJS   👄 💍 ⚠

Roman Kemp   ☐ ☐ ☐

Greg James   ☐ ☐ ☐

Nick Grimshaw   ☐ ☐ ☐

RADIO KINGS   👄 💍 ⚠

Chris Evans   ☐ ☐ ☐

Graham Norton   ☐ ☐ ☐

Michael Ball   ☐ ☐ ☐

TALK-SHOW LADS   👄 💍 ⚠

James Corden   ☐ ☐ ☐

Mo Gilligan   ☐ ☐ ☐

Big Narstie   ☐ ☐ ☐

TALK-SHOW LADIES

                                    👄 💍 ⚠

Oprah Winfrey ☐ ☐ ☐

Ellen DeGeneres ☐ ☐ ☐

Lorraine Kelly ☐ ☐ ☐

THE KARDASHIANS

                                    👄 💍 ⚠

Kim Kardashian-West ☐ ☐ ☐

Khloé Kardashian ☐ ☐ ☐

Kylie Jenner ☐ ☐ ☐

LOVABLE LADIES

                                    👄 💍 ⚠

Davina McCall ☐ ☐ ☐

Emma Willis ☐ ☐ ☐

Holly Willoughby ☐ ☐ ☐

'Nothing happens until you decide. Make a decision and watch your life move forward.'

OPRAH
WINFREY

TOWIE GALS

	👄	💍	⚠️
Gemma Collins	☐	☐	☐
Chloe Sims	☐	☐	☐
Sam Faiers	☐	☐	☐

TOWIE GUYS

	👄	💍	⚠️
Joey Essex	☐	☐	☐
Mark Wright	☐	☐	☐
James Argent	☐	☐	☐

MADE IN CHELSEA LADIES

	👄	💍	⚠️
Georgia Toffolo	☐	☐	☐
Alexandra Felstead	☐	☐	☐
Louise Thompson	☐	☐	☐

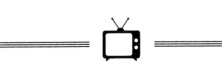

MADE IN CHELSEA LADS　　　👄 💍 ⚠

Jamie Laing ☐☐☐

Spencer Matthews ☐☐☐

Ollie Locke ☐☐☐

HAVING A LAUGH　　　👄 💍 ⚠

Romesh Ranganathan ☐☐☐

Joe Lycett ☐☐☐

James Acaster ☐☐☐

PANEL-SHOW QUEENS　　　👄 💍 ⚠

Katherine Ryan ☐☐☐

Sara Pascoe ☐☐☐

Aisling Bea ☐☐☐

GAME-SHOW HOSTS   👄 💍 ⚠️

Bradley Walsh ☐☐☐

Richard Osman ☐☐☐

Alexander Armstrong ☐☐☐

MOTD   👄 💍 ⚠️

Gary Lineker ☐☐☐

Alan Shearer ☐☐☐

Ian Wright ☐☐☐

THE VOICE LADS   👄 💍 ⚠️

will.i.am ☐☐☐

Tom Jones ☐☐☐

Danny O'Donoghue ☐☐☐

'I can't blow
my nose.
I've never
learned
how.'

JOEY ESSEX

THE VOICE LADIES

           👄 💍 ⚠️

Jessie J   ☐ ☐ ☐

Paloma Faith   ☐ ☐ ☐

Rita Ora   ☐ ☐ ☐

TV CHEFS

           👄 💍 ⚠️

Paul Hollywood   ☐ ☐ ☐

Gordon Ramsay   ☐ ☐ ☐

Jamie Oliver   ☐ ☐ ☐

BAKE-OFF BABES

           👄 💍 ⚠️

Mary Berry   ☐ ☐ ☐

Prue Leith   ☐ ☐ ☐

Sandi Toksvig   ☐ ☐ ☐

THIS MORNING MEN

👄 💍 ⚠

Phillip Schofield ☐ ☐ ☐

Eamonn Holmes ☐ ☐ ☐

Ben Shephard ☐ ☐ ☐

DYNAMIC DUOS

👄 💍 ⚠

Torvill and Dean ☐ ☐ ☐

Mel and Sue ☐ ☐ ☐

French and Saunders ☐ ☐ ☐

WOULD THEY LIE TO YOU?

👄 💍 ⚠

David Mitchell ☐ ☐ ☐

Rob Brydon ☐ ☐ ☐

Lee Mack ☐ ☐ ☐

EASTENDERS LADS

	👄	💍	⚠
Mick Carter	☐	☐	☐
Grant Mitchell	☐	☐	☐
Steve Owen	☐	☐	☐

EASTENDERS LADIES

	👄	💍	⚠
Bianca	☐	☐	☐
Kat Slater	☐	☐	☐
Tiffany Mitchell	☐	☐	☐

CORONATION STREET LADS

	👄	💍	⚠
Roy Cropper	☐	☐	☐
Kirk Sutherland	☐	☐	☐
Steve McDonald	☐	☐	☐

CORONATION STREET LADIES

👄 💍 ⚠

Michelle Connor ☐☐☐

Sarah Platt ☐☐☐

Maria Connor ☐☐☐

HOLLYOAKS GUYS

👄 💍 ⚠

Ste Hay ☐☐☐

Tony Hutchinson ☐☐☐

Calvin Valentine ☐☐☐

HOLLYOAKS GALS

👄 💍 ⚠

Sasha Valentine ☐☐☐

Hannah Ashworth ☐☐☐

Mercedes McQueen ☐☐☐

We all have secret crushes
– some are secret even to
ourselves! Often we can't
pinpoint why we feel the
way we do about somebody
– is it their confidence, their
style or just their joie de
vivre that we admire?

EXTRAS

                                                                     👄 💍 ⚠

Ricky Gervais ☐ ☐ ☐

Karl Pilkington ☐ ☐ ☐

Stephen Merchant ☐ ☐ ☐

JUDGES

  👄 💍 ⚠

David Walliams ☐ ☐ ☐

Simon Cowell ☐ ☐ ☐

Louis Walsh ☐ ☐ ☐

POLITICIANS

  👄 💍 ⚠

Nigel Farage ☐ ☐ ☐

Jacob Rees-Mogg ☐ ☐ ☐

Mark Francois ☐ ☐ ☐

PYTHONS

                                                    👄 💍 ⚠

Michael Palin

John Cleese

Eric Idle

8 OUT OF 10 CATS

👄 💍 ⚠

Jimmy Carr

Jon Richardson

Sean Lock

TOP GEAR

👄 💍 ⚠

Jeremy Clarkson

Richard Hammond

James May

MAGICIANS

👄 💍 ⚠️

Derren Brown

Dynamo

David Blaine

DOYENNES

👄 💍 ⚠️

Deborah Meaden

Anne Robinson

Anne Hegerty

ENTERTAINERS

👄 💍 ⚠️

Lenny Henry

Tim Minchin

Steve Carell

'BE HAPPY. IT REALLY ANNOYS NEGATIVE PEOPLE.'

RICKY GERVAIS

LOOSE WOMEN

	👄	💍	⚠
Kaye Adams	☐	☐	☐
Saira Khan	☐	☐	☐
Nadia Sawalha	☐	☐	☐

TV REGULARS

	👄	💍	⚠
Nick Knowles	☐	☐	☐
Phil Spencer	☐	☐	☐
Reggie Yates	☐	☐	☐

BIG PERSONALITIES

	👄	💍	⚠
Russell Brand	☐	☐	☐
Sacha Baron Cohen	☐	☐	☐
Keith Lemon	☐	☐	☐

WIZARDS

	👄	💍	⚠
Lucius Malfoy	☐	☐	☐
Severus Snape	☐	☐	☐
Sirius Black	☐	☐	☐

WESTMINSTER LADS

	👄	💍	⚠
George Osborne	☐	☐	☐
David Cameron	☐	☐	☐
Ken Livingstone	☐	☐	☐

COMEDY QUEENS

	👄	💍	⚠
Jennifer Saunders	☐	☐	☐
Dawn French	☐	☐	☐
Joanna Lumley	☐	☐	☐

COMEDY KINGS   👄 💍 ⚠

Seth Rogen   ☐ ☐ ☐

Jonah Hill   ☐ ☐ ☐

Bill Murray   ☐ ☐ ☐

GEEK CHIC   👄 💍 ⚠

Louis Theroux   ☐ ☐ ☐

Simon Pegg   ☐ ☐ ☐

Richard Ayoade   ☐ ☐ ☐

SPORT STARS   👄 💍 ⚠

Andy Murray   ☐ ☐ ☐

Gareth Bale   ☐ ☐ ☐

Tim Henman   ☐ ☐ ☐

'DEFINE YOURSELF BY WHAT YOU LOVE.'

TIM MINCHIN

?

The best thing to do in this round is answer quickly without overthinking it. Shag, Marry, Avoid becomes more of a Would You Rather game here, but just run with it and see what happens ...

FAST CARS

	👄	💍	⚠
Mercedes	☐	☐	☐
Jaguar	☐	☐	☐
Lamborghini	☐	☐	☐

BOOZY BEVERAGES

	👄	💍	⚠
Champagne	☐	☐	☐
Gin	☐	☐	☐
Prosecco	☐	☐	☐

DAYS OF THE WEEK

	👄	💍	⚠
Monday	☐	☐	☐
Friday	☐	☐	☐
Sunday	☐	☐	☐

FOOD, GLORIOUS FOOD

	👄	💍	⚠
Ice cream	☐	☐	☐
Roast dinner	☐	☐	☐
Big Mac	☐	☐	☐

COURSES

	👄	💍	⚠
Starter	☐	☐	☐
Main	☐	☐	☐
Dessert	☐	☐	☐

TAKE A SEAT

	👄	💍	⚠
Sofa	☐	☐	☐
Armchair	☐	☐	☐
Chaise longue	☐	☐	☐

?

ENGLISH BREAKFAST

👄 💍 ⚠

Eggs ☐☐☐

Sausage ☐☐☐

Hash brown ☐☐☐

RELAX TO THE MAX

👄 💍 ⚠

Hammock ☐☐☐

Bean bag ☐☐☐

Pouffe ☐☐☐

HOBBIES

👄 💍 ⚠

Books ☐☐☐

Films ☐☐☐

Music ☐☐☐

'I only drink champagne on two occasions: when I am in love and when I am not.'

COCO
CHANEL

?

COCKTAILS 👄 💍 ⚠️

Sex on the Beach ☐ ☐ ☐

Mojito ☐ ☐ ☐

Cosmopolitan ☐ ☐ ☐

DECORATION 👄 💍 ⚠️

Beard ☐ ☐ ☐

Tattoo ☐ ☐ ☐

Piercing ☐ ☐ ☐

EYE COLOUR 👄 💍 ⚠️

Blue ☐ ☐ ☐

Brown ☐ ☐ ☐

Green ☐ ☐ ☐

?

HOLIDAY ACTIVITIES 　　　　　👄 💍 ⚠

Sunbathing　　☐ ☐ ☐

Swimming　　☐ ☐ ☐

Reading　　☐ ☐ ☐

FOOTWEAR 　　　　　👄 💍 ⚠

Heels　　☐ ☐ ☐

Flats　　☐ ☐ ☐

Trainers　　☐ ☐ ☐

CLOTHES 　　　　　👄 💍 ⚠

Skirt　　☐ ☐ ☐

Trousers　　☐ ☐ ☐

Jeans　　☐ ☐ ☐

HOLIDAYS   👄 💍 ⚠

Sun, sea, sand ☐ ☐ ☐

City break ☐ ☐ ☐

Countryside retreat ☐ ☐ ☐

CELEBRATIONS   👄 💍 ⚠

Christmas ☐ ☐ ☐

Birthday ☐ ☐ ☐

Easter ☐ ☐ ☐

PRINTS AND PATTERNS   👄 💍 ⚠

Leopard ☐ ☐ ☐

Zebra ☐ ☐ ☐

Snakeskin ☐ ☐ ☐

'GIVE A GIRL
THE RIGHT PAIR
OF SHOES AND
SHE CAN
CONQUER THE
WORLD.'

MARILYN MONROE

?

BLT

	👄	💍	⚠️
Bacon	☐	☐	☐
Lettuce	☐	☐	☐
Tomato	☐	☐	☐

CAPTAINS

	👄	💍	⚠️
Captain Jack Sparrow	☐	☐	☐
Captain Hook	☐	☐	☐
Captain Birdseye	☐	☐	☐

DANCE ROUTINES

	👄	💍	⚠️
Macarena	☐	☐	☐
Gangnam Style	☐	☐	☐
Flossing	☐	☐	☐

CULTURAL NIGHT OUT

	👄	💍	⚠
Cinema			
Opera			
Ballet			

PLANETS

	👄	💍	⚠
Jupiter			
Mars			
Saturn			

TRANSPORT

	👄	💍	⚠
Train			
Plane			
Car			

CHEESE
⬿ 💍 ⚠

Halloumi	☐	☐	☐
Brie	☐	☐	☐
Cheddar	☐	☐	☐

SOCIALISING
⬿ 💍 ⚠

Big party	☐	☐	☐
Small gathering	☐	☐	☐
Intimate dinner	☐	☐	☐

MATERIAL
⬿ 💍 ⚠

Cotton	☐	☐	☐
Velvet	☐	☐	☐
Silk	☐	☐	☐

?

FIRST DATE   👄 💍 ⚠

	👄	💍	⚠
Bungee jump	☐	☐	☐
Long walk	☐	☐	☐
Classy restaurant	☐	☐	☐

WEDDING STYLE   👄 💍 ⚠

	👄	💍	⚠
Registry office	☐	☐	☐
Castle	☐	☐	☐
Elopement	☐	☐	☐

DANCE CLASS   👄 💍 ⚠

	👄	💍	⚠
Salsa	☐	☐	☐
Ballroom	☐	☐	☐
Hip-hop	☐	☐	☐

Friends & Acquaintances

Ever fantasised about your neighbour, your dentist or your local handyman? No? Well, here's your chance! There's even a space at the end of this chapter to add your own names and continue the fun!

AT WORK

Your boss

Your work spouse

Your office rival

AT HOME

Your neighbour

Your doctor

Your MP

YOUR PEERS

Your best friend

Your frenemy

Your nemesis

'True friends
say good things
behind your back
and bad things to
your face.'

UNKNOWN

YOUR FIRST ...

       👄 💍 ⚠

Kiss

Crush

Love

YOUR BEST FRIEND'S ...

       👄 💍 ⚠

Sibling

Cousin

Partner

SCHOOL DAYS

       👄 💍 ⚠

Your favourite teacher

Your headteacher

Your funniest teacher

'Ever looked
at your ex and
wondered,
"Was I drunk
the entire
relationship?"'

UNKNOWN

CLASSROOM CHARACTERS

	👄	💍	⚠
The class clown	☐	☐	☐
The class brainiac	☐	☐	☐
The class hottie	☐	☐	☐

FRIENDS WITH BENEFITS

	👄	💍	⚠
Your sporty friend	☐	☐	☐
Your flirty friend	☐	☐	☐
Your awkward friend	☐	☐	☐

PERSONALITY TRAITS

	👄	💍	⚠
Confident	☐	☐	☐
Shy	☐	☐	☐
Funny	☐	☐	☐

EXES
⬧ ⌖ ⚠

Your ex ☐ ☐ ☐

Your ex ex ☐ ☐ ☐

Your ex ex ex ☐ ☐ ☐

LOCAL PEOPLE
⬧ ⌖ ⚠

Your mayor ☐ ☐ ☐

Your postal worker ☐ ☐ ☐

Your dentist ☐ ☐ ☐

WHO YOU GONNA CALL?
⬧ ⌖ ⚠

Your handyman ☐ ☐ ☐

Your plumber ☐ ☐ ☐

Your window cleaner ☐ ☐ ☐

Use This Space to Add Your Own!

_____ ⦳ ŏ ⚠

.... ☐ ☐ ☐
.... ☐ ☐ ☐
.... ☐ ☐ ☐

_____ ⦳ ŏ ⚠

.... ☐ ☐ ☐
.... ☐ ☐ ☐
.... ☐ ☐ ☐

_____ ⦳ ŏ ⚠

.... ☐ ☐ ☐
.... ☐ ☐ ☐
.... ☐ ☐ ☐

_____   👄 💍 ⚠️

.... ☐ ☐ ☐

.... ☐ ☐ ☐

.... ☐ ☐ ☐

_____   👄 💍 ⚠️

.... ☐ ☐ ☐

.... ☐ ☐ ☐

.... ☐ ☐ ☐

_____   👄 💍 ⚠️

.... ☐ ☐ ☐

.... ☐ ☐ ☐

.... ☐ ☐ ☐